THE ULTIMATE
BOOK OF
KID CONCOCTIONS

More Than 65 Wacky, Wild, & Crazy Concoctions

John E. & Danita Thomas

B&H
PUBLISHING GROUP
Nashville, Tennessee

D1530587

Ten-digit ISBN: 0-8054-4443-2
Thirteen-digit ISBN: 978-0-8054-4443-8

Published by B&H Publishing Group, Nashville, Tennessee

Dewey Decimal Classification: 372.5
Subject Heading: CREATIVE ACTIVITIES \ HANDICRAFT

Authors are represented by the literary agency of Nashville Agency,
P. O. Box 110909, Nashville, Tennessee 37222.

CREDITS:
Cover art design: Robert Durr
Cover photography: Bill Dragga
Illustrations: Robb Durr and Zachariah Durr

Authors' Web site: www.kidconcoctions.com
Publisher's Web site: www.BHPublishingGroup.com

1 2 3 4 5 6 7 8 9 10   10 09 08 07 06

Dedications

John's dedications:

To my parents, Gloria and Grover Thomas, who always believed in my dreams.

To my business partner and dearest friend, Danita, who always manages to put a smile on my face and in my heart.

Danita's dedications:

To my precious children, Kyle, Kalie, and Kellen, who are the dearest blessings in my life.
To my loving family, thank you for all your love and support and all you've done for me.

To John, my creative inspiration, whose friendship, faithfulness, and respect mean the world to me. I thank you for sharing so much. This book is one of many dreams come true.

Acknowledgments

We would like to thank the people, whose valuable contributions made this book possible.

We would also like to thank the many people who responded to our television appearances through the years and requested we write a book just like this one . . . here it is!

Foreword

In the years since we first created the Kid Concoctions projects to help us teach Sunday school classes, many parents have told us that they want to spend time enjoying crafts with their children but that it is difficult to find inexpensive, high-quality projects their children will enjoy. It is our hope that this book will provide you and your children with many hours of amusement and amazement together.

The Ultimate Book of Kid Concoctions takes children's arts and crafts to a whole new level with fresh ideas for creating the very best in children's concoctions, crafts, and toys. Our easy-to-follow recipes let children take pride and satisfaction in creating superior projects, regardless of their experience or artistic ability. *The Ultimate Book of Kid Concoctions* will encourage your child to explore, create, learn, and experiment.

We have written this book with the hope that you will "concoct" along with your child. More than anything, your child wants and needs your time, love, and attention. Many of our fondest memories are those we've made doing fun projects like these with our own children. Your child is only a "kid" for a short season of his or her life. Enjoy these fun and playful days, for they are priceless. Many years from now, your child will think back on the happy memories you create today, and maybe they will be inspired to make new memories like these with their own children someday.

May God bless you and your family. Happy concocting!

John E. Thomas & Danita Thomas

CONTENTS

Adult supervision is recommended for all projects and recipes, especially those using a stove, oven, microwave, or glue gun. Some ingredients used in these recipes, such as Borax, liquid bluing, plaster of Paris, and quick dry cement should be handled only by adults wearing protective gloves.

GOOEY GUNK

This slimy, stretchy, gooey recipe has become one of the most popular concoctions of all time.

WHAT YOU WILL NEED:

Solution A
- 1 cup water
- 1 cup white glue
- 2 Tbs. liquid tempera paint or 7 to 10 drops food coloring

Solution B
- 1 1/3 cups warm water
- 4 tsp. Borax laundry booster

HOW TO CONCOCT IT:

1. Mix ingredients from Solution A together in a medium bowl.
2. In a second medium bowl, mix the ingredients from Solution B together until the Borax is completely dissolved.
3. Slowly pour Solution A into Solution B (Do not mix!).
4. Roll Solution A around in Solution B 4 to 5 times.
5. Lift Solution A out of Solution B and knead for 2 to 3 minutes.
6. Store Gooey Gunk in an airtight container or plastic ziplock bag.

CONCOCTION TIPS & IDEAS:

◆ Use red liquid tempera paint/food coloring to create Lava Gunk, green to create Slimy Gunk, or black to create Tar Gunk.

WATER BALLOON YO-YO

Try this unusual outdoor yo-yo to provide hours of fun. It always seems to bounce right back.

WHAT YOU WILL NEED:

1 small balloon
1 large rubber band

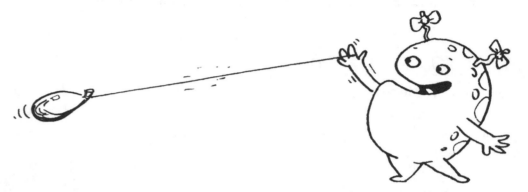

HOW TO CONCOCT IT:

1. Cut the rubber band in half.
2. Tie a loop securely on one end of the rubber band. It should be big enough to fit around your finger.
3. Use a garden hose or water faucet to fill the balloon 1/4 of the way with water.
4. Blow air into the balloon until it is the size of a tennis ball. Tie the balloon shut.
5. Securely tie the rubber band around the knot on the balloon.
6. Place the rubber band loop around your middle finger and gently throw the balloon toward the ground. When the balloon springs back toward your hand, try to grab it.

CONCOCTION TIPS & IDEAS:

◆ Use the Water Balloon Yo-Yo to put a twist on classic yo-yo tricks like Rock the Cradle and Around the World. You can also experiment and create brand new tricks of your very own.
◆ Use colored markers and stickers to decorate and personalize your Water Balloon Yo-Yo.

SCRATCH & SNIFF WATERCOLORS

With *Scratch & Sniff Watercolors* you can paint pictures of oranges that smell like oranges, grapes that smell like grapes, and cherries that smell like cherries.

WHAT YOU WILL NEED:

1 Tbs. unsweetened powdered drink mix
1 Tbs. warm water
Several small containers (muffin tins work well)

HOW TO CONCOCT IT:

1. Mix water and unsweetened powdered drink mix together in a small bowl. Repeat this step several times, using various flavors of drink mix to create different colors of paint.
2. Allow finished works to dry overnight before scratching and sniffing.

CONCOCTION TIPS & IDEAS:

◆ Use Scratch & Sniff Watercolors along with the Make-It-Yourself Stickers recipe to create your very own Scratch & Sniff stickers.
◆ Create unique Scratch & Sniff greeting cards and wrapping paper.

SPARKLE BOTTLE

Metallic glitter is magically suspended in plastic soda bottles, creating a rainbow of swirling colors.

WHAT YOU WILL NEED:

Small clear, plastic soda bottle with a cap
Light corn syrup
Assorted shapes of metallic confetti (found in gift and card shops)
Cold water

HOW TO CONCOCT IT:

1. Fill soda bottle 3/4 of the way with corn syrup.
2. Add a small handful of metallic confetti.
3. Top the bottle off with water.
4. Seal the bottle securely with a cap and shake.

CONCOCTION TIPS & IDEAS:

◆ Add a few drops of food coloring to your Sparkle Bottle for added interest.
◆ Create Sparkle Wands by using a 1-inch diameter clear plastic aquarium lift tube (found in pet supply stores) and two 1-inch plastic chair leg caps (found in hardware stores). Secure a plastic chair leg cap on one end of the lift tube with a hot glue gun. Fill the tube with corn syrup, glitter, and cold water. Glue the remaining chair leg cap on the other end of the tube and shake.

BATHTUB FINGER PAINTS

You'll have fun finger painting while getting yourself and the tub clean at the same time.

WHAT YOU WILL NEED:

1/3 cup clear, liquid dish detergent
1 Tbs. cornstarch
Food coloring

HOW TO CONCOCT IT:

1. Mix liquid dish detergent and cornstarch together in a small bowl until blended.
2. Pour the mixture, in equal parts, into several sections of a plastic ice cube tray.
3. Add 1 to 2 drops of food coloring to each section of the tray and mix with a small spoon.

CONCOCTION TIPS & IDEAS:

◆ Use Bathtub Finger Paints on the inside or outside of the bathtub to paint pictures and even play games such as Hangman and Tic-Tac-Toe.
◆ Bathtub Finger Paints also work well as a traditional finger paint.

RAINBOW SAND

Use this fun and inexpensive alternative to craft store art sand.

WHAT YOU WILL NEED:

1 cup sand or table salt
2 tsp. powdered tempera paint
Plastic ziplock bag

HOW TO CONCOCT IT:

1. Pour sand or table salt and powdered tempera paint into a ziplock bag.
   Shake bag for 30 seconds or until the color is evenly blended.
2. Repeat the above step several times to create different colors of Rainbow Sand.
3. Store leftover sand in a ziplock bag or in an airtight container.

CONCOCTION TIPS & IDEAS:

◆ Layer different colors of Rainbow Sand in a small, clear plastic soda bottle to create sand art bottles.
◆ Draw a picture or outline a picture in a coloring book using white glue. Sprinkle different colors of
   Rainbow Sand over the picture to create really cool 3-D sand paintings.

FUNNY PUTTY

This stretchy, rubbery putty bounces like a ball and picks up newspaper comics.

WHAT YOU WILL NEED:

1 Tbs. liquid starch
Food coloring
2 Tbs. white glue
Plastic Easter egg or plastic ziplock bag

HOW TO CONCOCT IT:

1. Mix white glue and 2 to 3 drops of food coloring together in a small bowl.
2. Pour liquid starch into a second small bowl. Slowly pour the glue mixture on top of the liquid starch.
3. Allow the concoction to stand for 5 minutes or until the glue absorbs the liquid starch.
4. Remove putty from bowl and knead. (Note: At first this mixture may look as if it's a mistake, but it isn't. The more you knead the putty, the better the consistency will be.)
5. Store Funny Putty in a plastic Easter egg or ziplock bag.

CONCOCTION TIPS & IDEAS:

◆ Press Funny Putty down on newspaper comics or pictures printed with an ink jet printer. Slowly pull the Funny Putty off the paper. The picture will transfer magically onto the putty.
◆ Roll your Funny Putty into a ball and bounce it!

TROPICAL RAIN STICK

Traditional rain sticks are often made of cactus or bamboo, but with this concoction you can quickly and easily make a rain stick from common household items.

WHAT YOU WILL NEED:

Heavy cardboard mailing tube
2 plastic caps or duct tape to seal the tube
Nails
Hammer
Seeds, small pebbles, rice, or dried beans
Adhesive-backed shelf paper, wrapping paper, or ribbon

HOW TO CONCOCT IT:

1. Hammer nails into the mailing tube 1/8-inch apart, using the spiral seam of the cardboard tube as a guide.
2. Add several handfuls of assorted filler material (rice, seeds, beans, etc.).
3. Seal each end of the tube securely with plastic caps or duct tape.
4. Decorate your Tropical Rain Stick with ribbon, adhesive-backed shelf paper, or wrapping paper.

CONCOCTION TIPS & IDEAS:

◆ Use your Tropical Rain Stick as a musical instrument. Shake it and twist it to create a wide variety of different sounds.

SUPER SIDEWALK PAINT

Now you can color large portions of sidewalk space in just a fraction of the time it would take with traditional stick chalk.

WHAT YOU WILL NEED:

1/4 cup cornstarch
1/4 cup cold water
Food coloring

HOW TO CONCOCT IT:

1. Mix cornstarch and cold water together in a small plastic bowl.
2. Add 6 to 8 drops of food coloring and stir.
3. Repeat this process to create different colors of Super Sidewalk Paint.
   (Super Sidewalk Paint can easily be washed away with water.)

CONCOCTION TIPS & IDEAS:

◆ Super Sidewalk Paint is great for painting rainbows or other pictures where large areas of color are needed.
◆ Use Super Sidewalk Paint for painting hopscotch grids, cakewalks, even make-believe roads and highways for toy cars.

MAGIC MUCK

This *mysterious concoction* turns from a liquid into a solid and back again.

WHAT YOU WILL NEED:

3/4 cup cornstarch
1/3 cup water
Food coloring

HOW TO CONCOCT IT:

1. Mix water and 5 to 7 drops of food coloring together in a small bowl.
2. Slowly add cornstarch to water and food coloring mixture.
   Do not stir!
3. Let the mixture stand for 2 to 3 minutes.
4. Pick up a handful of Magic Muck and squeeze it until it forms a hard ball.
   Open your hand and the Magic Muck will turn from a solid ball back into a liquid.

CONCOCTION TIPS & IDEAS:

◆ Experiment by adding different proportions of water and cornstarch.
◆ Add a little glitter to make your Magic Muck sparkle.

PAPER CLAY

Paper Clay is a fabulous molding compound that will allow you to sculpt and mold, using real paper.

WHAT YOU WILL NEED:

2 cups construction paper scraps (sorted by color)
4 1/2 cups water
1/2 cup flour

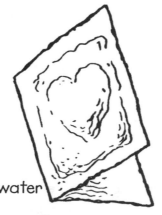

HOW TO CONCOCT IT:

1. Tear construction paper into small pieces. Pour 4 cups water and paper scraps into a blender. Blend 20 seconds or until the mixture turns to a pulp.
2. Drain and squeeze excess water from the mixture.
3. Mix flour and the remaining 1/2 cup of water in a small bowl until blended.
4. Slowly add the flour and water mixture to paper pulp. Knead until it forms a dough.
5. Mold Paper Clay as you would any clay or dough. Let finished creations dry 1 to 2 days.

CONCOCTION TIPS & IDEAS:

◆ Paper Clay can be used to create 3-D greeting cards, pictures, package ties, or tree ornaments.
◆ Try adding glitter or bits of confetti to your Paper Clay.
◆ Press Paper Clay into candy molds, cookie cutters, or gelatin molds to create interesting shapes.

PUDDIN' PAINT

Budding young artists will enjoy this wonderful "first paint."

WHAT YOU WILL NEED:

1 large package of instant vanilla pudding (3.4 oz)
2 cups ice-cold water
Food coloring

HOW TO CONCOCT IT:

1. Whisk water and instant vanilla pudding together in a bowl for 2 minutes.
2. Refrigerate for 5 minutes.
3. Divide pudding into several small bowls or muffin tins.
4. Add 5 to 7 drops of food coloring to each bowl or tin and mix.

CONCOCTION TIPS & IDEAS:

◆ Use Puddin' Paint along with other paints in this book to create really cool works of art.
◆ Puddin' Paints can also double as fantastic finger paint!

FANTASY FOSSILS

These make-believe fossils look and feel as if they're real!

WHAT YOU WILL NEED:

2 cups quick-setting plaster of Paris
1 cup water
Sand

HOW TO CONCOCT IT:

1. Fill a pan or bowl with sand. Sprinkle the sand lightly
   with water until it is moist enough to hold an impression.
2. Make an impression in the sand, using hard objects such
   as a shell, a rubber lizard, or even your own hand!
3. Mix water and quick-setting plaster together in a small bowl.
4. Immediately pour the plaster mixture into sand impression.
   Be careful not to let the plaster touch the edge of the pan or the fossil will be difficult to remove.
5. Let the plaster dry for 35 to 45 minutes or until hard.
6. Remove fossil from sand.

CONCOCTION TIPS & IDEAS:

◆ Create color-tinted Fantasy Fossils by mixing in 1 Tbs. of powdered tempera paint to the plaster
   before adding water.

TATTOO PAINT

This rich, creamy paint allows you to create colorful, removable tattoos.

WHAT YOU WILL NEED:

1 Tbs. cold cream
2 Tbs. cornstarch
1 Tbs. water
Food coloring

HOW TO CONCOCT IT:

1. Mix cold cream and cornstarch together in a small bowl.
   Stir in water. Continue stirring until the mixture is smooth.
2. Divide the mixture into 3 or 4 small plastic bowls.
3. Mix 3 to 4 drops of food coloring into each bowl.
4. Apply Tattoo Paint using a small paint brush or cotton swab.
5. Remove paint with soap and water.

CONCOCTION TIPS & IDEAS:

◆ Use Tattoo Paint to create removable tattoos on your arms, legs, and face.
◆ Tattoo Paint works well when used in conjunction with Face & Body Paint to create different characters.

SPLONGEE BALL

This soft starburst-shaped ball is fun to play with indoors or out.

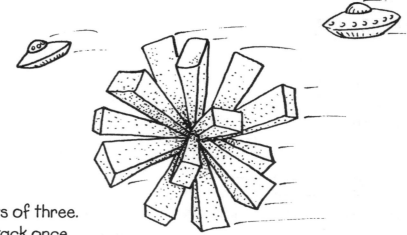

WHAT YOU WILL NEED:

3 large sponges (Use 3 different colored sponges.)
1 plastic cable tie
Scissors

HOW TO CONCOCT IT:

1. Cut each sponge into thirds lengthwise.
2. Stack the cut sponges on top of each other in three rows of three.
3. Grab the stack of sponges in the center and twist the stack once.
4. Secure a plastic cable tie around the center of the twisted stack, pulling it as tight as possible.
5. Trim the plastic cable tie down as close to the eye as possible.

CONCOCTION TIPS & IDEAS:

◆ Use nylon sponges. They stay soft, cost less, and come in a wide variety of colors.
◆ Wet your Splongee Ball and take it outside to play a splashy game of toss.
◆ Use Splongee Ball to play soccer or volleyball.

PEANUTTY PLAY DOUGH

Here's a great dough for sculpting edible works of art.

WHAT YOU WILL NEED:

1/4 cup peanut butter
1/2 cup non-fat dry milk
1/2 Tbs. honey
Plastic ziplock bag

HOW TO CONCOCT IT:

1. Pour peanut butter, dry milk, and honey into a ziplock bag.
2. Close bag and knead until the mixture turns to dough.
3. Do not reuse or store Peanutty Play Dough.

CONCOCTION TIPS & IDEAS:

◆ Use Peanutty Play Dough to create a wide variety of edible sculptures including animals, flowers, and even dinosaurs.
◆ Use raisins and assorted candies to add eyes, mouths, and other features to your edible creations.

INVISIBLE INK

With this easy ink recipe, you can write secret messages that are visible only when exposed to heat.

WHAT YOU WILL NEED:

2 Tbs. pure lemon juice
Cotton swab

HOW TO CONCOCT IT:

1. Pour lemon juice into a small glass or plastic dish.
2. Soak one end of the cotton swab in the lemon juice.
3. Use the lemon juice-soaked swab to write a secret message
   or draw a picture on a sheet of paper.
4. When you are ready to view your secret message, have an adult
   hold the sheet of paper near a light bulb or over a toaster.
   The heat source will slowly turn the lemon juice dark brown and reveal the message.

CONCOCTION TIPS & IDEAS:

◆ Create a secret treasure map using Invisible Ink.
◆ Write top-secret notes and messages that only your friends can read.

MAGIC BUBBLE PAINT

Use this concoction to create and capture bright, colorful bubble prints.

WHAT YOU WILL NEED:

2 tsp. clear, liquid dish detergent
3 Tbs. water
1/4 cup powdered tempera paint

HOW TO CONCOCT IT:

1. Mix clear, liquid dish detergent, water, and powdered tempera paint together in a small shallow bowl. If you are using concentrated dish detergent, 1 to 2 more Tbs. of water may be necessary.
2. Using a straw, gently blow into the paint mixture until a dome of bubbles forms. (Don't drink it!)
3. Capture bubble prints by placing a piece of paper on top of the bubble dome.
4. Repeat the process, using several different colors of bubble paint.

CONCOCTION TIPS & IDEAS:

◆ Use Magic Bubble Paint to create custom stationery, envelopes, greeting cards, wrapping paper, photo mats, and cool lunch bags.
◆ Layer different colors of Magic Bubble Paint to create a swirling "marble-like" effect.

OATMEAL PLAY CLAY

Oatmeal Play Clay's interesting texture provides a unique sculpting experience for kids of all ages.

WHAT YOU WILL NEED:

1/2 cup flour
1/2 cup water
1 cup oatmeal

HOW TO CONCOCT IT:

1. Combine flour, water, and oatmeal together in a medium bowl.
2. Stir until the mixture is smooth. If the dough is too sticky, add more flour.
3. Remove Oatmeal Play Clay from the bowl and place it on a floured surface.
4. Knead dough for 3 to 4 minutes. Store in an airtight container.

CONCOCTION TIPS & IDEAS:

◆ Make different colors of Oatmeal Play Clay by stirring 6 to 8 drops of food coloring into the dough mixture.
◆ Oatmeal Play Clay is the perfect dough recipe for a young child's first sculpting experience.

PAPIER-MÂCHÉ PASTE

This classic concoction recipe has been a favorite of children for many years.

WHAT YOU WILL NEED:

1 cup cold water
1/4 cup flour
5 cups water

HOW TO CONCOCT IT:

1. Mix flour and 1 cup cold water in a small bowl until smooth.
2. Heat 5 cups of water in a large saucepan over medium heat until the water begins to boil.
3. Add flour and water mixture to boiling water. Continue to boil, while constantly stirring for 3 to 5 minutes.
4. Remove pan from heat and allow Papier-Mâché Paste to cool.
5. Dip strips of newspaper in Papier-Mâché Paste and place them over some type of mold or form (i.e., balloon or box).
6. Allow finished papier-mâché sculptures to dry overnight or until hard.

CONCOCTION TIPS & IDEAS:

◆ Create a piñata by covering a large balloon with several layers of newspaper strips dipped in Papier-Mâché Paste. After the newspaper strips have dried, pop the balloon and fill the empty cavity with candy and toy prizes. Seal the hole with duct tape and decorate the piñata with paint, markers, streamers, and crepe paper. Suspend the piñata and take turns with your friends trying to hit it with a stick while blindfolded. Eventually the piñata will break open, releasing candy and toy prizes.

OCEAN IN A BOTTLE

Ocean in a Bottle captures the look of rumbling ocean waves in a small, hand-held bottle.

WHAT YOU WILL NEED:

1 clear plastic 16 oz. soda bottle with a cap
3/4 cup light cooking oil
1/2 Tbs. blue, powdered tempera paint
Water
Funnel

HOW TO CONCOCT IT:

1. Mix oil and blue powdered tempera paint together in a bowl.
2. Let the mixture set for 10 minutes. This allows any powdered tempera paint that has not dissolved to settle at the bottom of the bowl.
3. Using the funnel, slowly pour the oil into the plastic soda bottle. Do not pour the sediment at the bottom of the bowl into the bottle!
4. Using the funnel, pour water into the bottle until it is full.
5. Screw the cap on the bottle tightly. Slowly tilt the Ocean in a Bottle right to left and watch as the waves crash against the sides of the bottle.

CONCOCTION TIPS & IDEAS:

◆ Substitute red powdered tempera paint in place of the blue to create Lava in a Bottle.
◆ Use bottles of assorted sizes and shapes to create interesting Ocean/Lava effects.

I CAN'T BELIEVE IT'S NOT OIL PAINT

Here's a concoction that captures the look and feel of real oil paint without the expense or mess!

WHAT YOU WILL NEED:

2 Tbs. clear, liquid dishwashing detergent
2 Tbs. powdered tempera paint
1/2 tsp. water

HOW TO CONCOCT IT:

1. Pour liquid dishwashing detergent, powdered tempera paint, and water into a small bowl or container.
2. Mix the ingredients together until completely blended.
3. I Can't Believe It's Not Oil Paint can be stored for several weeks at room temperature in an airtight container.

CONCOCTION TIPS & IDEAS:

◆ Mix different colors of I Can't Believe It's Not Oil Paint together to create your own unique custom-blended paints.
◆ Think of names to call all the new colors you've created, even silly names such as Orangutan Orange or Stoplight Red.

FRUITY LIP GLOSS

You can make this tasty lip gloss at home, using nothing more than common kitchen ingredients.

WHAT YOU WILL NEED:

2 Tbs. solid shortening
1 Tbs. fruit-flavored powdered drink mix
35 mm-plastic film container (unused or well-washed)

HOW TO CONCOCT IT:

1. Mix shortening and drink mix together in a small microwave-safe container until smooth.
2. Place container in the microwave on High for 30 seconds until mixture becomes a liquid.
3. Pour the mixture into a well-washed plastic film container or any other type of small airtight container.
4. Place the Fruity Lip Gloss mixture in the refrigerator for 20 to 30 minutes or until firm.

CONCOCTION TIPS & IDEAS:

◆ Decorate your Fruity Lip Gloss container by using markers, glitter, or adhesive-backed shelf paper.
◆ Create a Fruity Lip Gloss necklace by placing an O-ring (found in any hardware store) around a plastic film container filled with Fruity Lip Gloss. Tie a piece of yarn or string to the O-ring.

WORLD'S BEST BUBBLES

After testing dozens of bubble recipes, we found this one to be the best of the best.

WHAT YOU WILL NEED:

2 1/2 qts. water
1/2 cup light corn syrup
1 cup liquid dish detergent

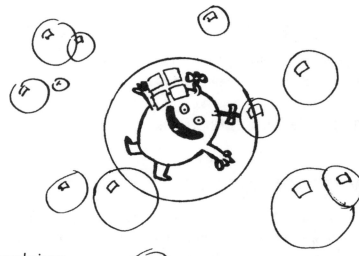

HOW TO CONCOCT IT:

1. Mix water and corn syrup together until completely blended.
2. Gently stir in the liquid dish detergent.
3. World's Best Bubbles will store for several weeks in an airtight container.

CONCOCTION TIPS & IDEAS:

◆ Add a little color to your bubbles by stirring in a few drops of food coloring.
◆ Create bubbles in many different sizes by dipping various items such as a plastic strawberry basket or wire whisk into the bubble solution.

SIDEWALK CHALK

With this concoction, you can create any size, color, and shape of Sidewalk Chalk imaginable.

WHAT YOU WILL NEED:

1/3 cup quick-setting plaster of Paris
1 Tbs. powdered tempera paint
3 Tbs. water
Plastic cookie cutter, candy mold, or toilet paper tube

HOW TO CONCOCT IT:

1. Mix plaster, powdered tempera paint, and water together in a small bowl until blended.
2. Quickly spoon the mixture into a cookie cutter, candy mold, or toilet paper tube
   sealed at one end with duct tape.
3. Let the chalk dry 30 to 45 minutes.
4. Carefully pop the chalk out of the cookie cutter or candy mold.
   If you are using a toilet paper tube, peel the tube away from the stick of chalk.

CONCOCTION TIPS & IDEAS:

◆ You can create Sidewalk Chalk in a wide assortment of shapes by using different plastic molds such as ice cube trays and paper cups.
◆ Try adding 1 tsp. of glitter to the plaster before adding water to make your chalk sparkle.

TORNADO IN A BOTTLE

This simple concoction creates an amazingly realistic miniature tornado.

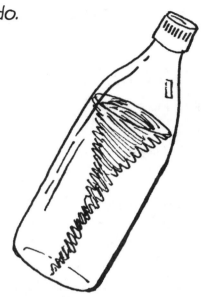

WHAT YOU WILL NEED:

1 clear plastic 16 oz. soda bottle with a cap (The more round the bottle,
   the better the tornado will work.)
2 drops clear, liquid dish detergent
1 tsp. glitter
Cold water

HOW TO CONCOCT IT:

1. Fill clear, plastic 16 oz. bottle with cold water.
2. Add liquid dish detergent and glitter to the bottle.
3. Screw the cap on the bottle tightly.
4. Holding the bottle by the neck turn it upside down. Quickly rotate your wrist
   several times in a clockwise motion. When you stop rotating your wrist, a mini-tornado
   will form inside the bottle.

CONCOCTION TIPS & IDEAS:

◆ Using permanent markers, draw a picture of a city or landscape around the bottom of the plastic bottle.
◆ Add a few drops of blue food coloring to the bottle to create a sky effect.

FOAMY PAINT

Foamy paint is not just great for painting on paper. You can also use it to paint on tile floors and walls.

WHAT YOU WILL NEED:

1 can white shaving cream
Food coloring
Plastic ice cube tray or muffin tin

HOW TO CONCOCT IT:

1. Place a small dab of shaving cream into several ice cube tray or muffin tin sections.
2. Add 1 to 2 drops of food coloring to each section and mix with a small spoon.

CONCOCTION TIPS & IDEAS:

◆ Use Foamy Paint to create 3-D foam sculptures.
◆ Foamy Paint can be used to paint pictures on your arms and legs.

WOODY WOOD DOUGH

With this amazing concoction, you can create and mold real wood sculptures in just a few minutes.

WHAT YOU WILL NEED:

1 cup clean, well-sifted sawdust
1/2 cup flour
1 Tbs. liquid starch
1 cup water

HOW TO CONCOCT IT:

1. Mix ingredients together in bowl until a stiff dough is formed.
   Add extra water if dough is too dry. Mold or sculpt into amazing creations.
2. Allow Woody Wood Dough to dry 2 to 3 days. Sandpaper can be used to smooth Woody Wood Dough after it is completely dry.

CONCOCTION TIPS & IDEAS:

◆ Press Woody Wood Dough into cookie cutters and candy molds to create paperweights, beads, and tree ornaments.
◆ Finished pieces can be painted or stained with a mixture of food coloring and water (6 drops of food coloring to 1 Tbs. of water).

MAKE-IT-YOURSELF STICKERS

Set your creativity free to make any size or shape sticker design imaginable.

WHAT YOU WILL NEED:

4 Tbs. hot water
2 Tbs. flavored gelatin

HOW TO CONCOCT IT:

1. Pour gelatin in a small glass bowl. Add hot water and stir until blended.
2. Brush mixture on the back of a small picture, drawing, or magazine cut-out.
3. Allow the sticker to set for 30 to 45 minutes or until dry.
4. When you're ready to use your sticker, just wet the back and then stick it.

CONCOCTION TIPS & IDEAS:

◆ Create your very own sticker album by stapling together several sheets of paper. You can then decorate the cover with crayons, markers, or even your favorite stickers.

INSTANT FINGER PAINTS

With this quick and easy concoction, you can duplicate commercial-quality finger paints.

WHAT YOU WILL NEED:

1/4 cup liquid starch
1 Tbs. powdered tempera paint
Freezer paper (Paint on the shiny side.)

HOW TO CONCOCT IT:

1. Pour liquid starch and powdered tempera paint into a small bowl.
2. Mix until well-blended.
3. Use plastic margarine tubs with lids to store finger paints for future use.

CONCOCTION TIPS & IDEAS:

◆ Create pictures of all your favorite people, places, and things. You may even want to challenge a friend or family member to a game of Instant Finger Paint Tic-Tac-Toe!
◆ Use a brush to paint with Instant Finger Paints just as you would any other paint.

SQUISHY BALL

This squishy ball will stretch and mold into different shapes and sizes.

WHAT YOU WILL NEED:

1 medium-sized balloon
1/2 cup sand or salt
Funnel

HOW TO CONCOCT IT:

1. Place balloon over the end of a funnel.
2. Pour 1/2 cup sand or salt into the funnel. If the entire 1/2 cup of filler
   doesn't seem to fit into the balloon, use a straw or the eraser end of a pencil
   to force the remaining filler into the balloon.
3. Squeeze out any air that may have become trapped in the balloon. Tie the balloon shut.

CONCOCTION TIPS & IDEAS:

◆ Use different filler ingredients such as cornstarch, flour, or rice to give Squishy Balls a completely different feel.
◆ Squishy Balls can be used for juggling or just for playing catch with a friend.

PLASTIC DOUGH

This stretchy, moldable dough quickly dries to a hard, plastic-like consistency.

WHAT YOU WILL NEED:

Food coloring
1/4 cup white glue
1/2 cup flour
1/2 cup cornstarch
1/4 cup water

HOW TO CONCOCT IT:

1. Mix white glue, water, and 4 to 6 drops of food coloring together
   in a small bowl until well-blended.
2. Combine flour and cornstarch in a separate bowl.
3. Add the flour/cornstarch mixture to the water/glue mixture. Mix until a stiff dough is formed.
4. Remove dough from the bowl and knead on a floured surface for 2 to 3 minutes.
5. Mold plastic dough on a surface covered with wax paper. Drying time will vary according
   to the size and thickness of your creation.

CONCOCTION TIPS & IDEAS:

◆ Plastic Dough can be used to create a wide variety of different items, including beads, jewelry, paperweights,
   bookmarks, or anything else your imagination will allow.

KOOKIE CREEPIES

Here's a no-bake concoction very similar to an expensive toy store solution used to create rubber-like creatures.

WHAT YOU WILL NEED:

1 envelope unflavored gelatin
2 Tbs. hot water
2 Tbs. white glue
1/2 Tbs. liquid tempera paint
Assorted candy molds
Plastic ziplock bag

HOW TO CONCOCT IT:

1. Mix liquid tempera paint and white glue together in a small bowl.
2. In another small bowl, mix gelatin and hot water together until gelatin is completely dissolved.
3. Add the gelatin/water mixture to the glue/paint mixture.
4. Stir until the concoction begins to thicken. This can take as long as 6 to 7 minutes.
5. When the mixture thickens, quickly pour it into a candy mold or cookie cutter.
6. Place the mold in the freezer for 5 minutes or until firm.
7. Carefully remove Kookie Creepies from the candy molds or cookie cutters and allow them to dry for 1 hour on each side. Store in an airtight ziplock bag.

CONCOCTION TIPS & IDEAS:

◆ Play with Kookie Creepies just as you would any other kind of rubber-type creature.
◆ Allow Kookie Creepies to air dry for 2 to 3 days, and they will transform into hard, plastic-like creatures.

FACE & BODY PAINT

Here's a wonderful face and body paint that is very similar to store-bought grease paint makeup.

WHAT YOU WILL NEED:

2 Tbs. solid shortening
1 Tbs. cornstarch
Food coloring
Small makeup sponges

HOW TO CONCOCT IT:

1. Mix shortening and cornstarch together in a small bowl until smooth.
2. Add 4 to 6 drops of food coloring. Mix until the color is evenly blended.
3. Apply Face & Body Paint to arms, legs, and face, using a small makeup sponge.
4. Remove paint with soap and water.

CONCOCTION TIPS & IDEAS:

◆ Children can use Face & Body Paint to transform themselves into green spacemen, or even circus clowns.
◆ Add 1 tsp. of glitter to Face & Body Paint to create sparkle makeup.

JAVA DOUGH

This silky, smooth dough smells like fresh-brewed coffee and dries to an antique finish.

WHAT YOU WILL NEED:

1/4 cup instant coffee
3/4 cup warm water
2 cups flour
1/2 cup salt
Airtight container or plastic ziplock bag

HOW TO CONCOCT IT:

1. Mix water and instant coffee together until the instant coffee is dissolved.
2. Combine flour and salt in a medium bowl.
3. Add water and coffee mixture and stir until a smooth dough is formed.
4. Bake finished sculptures in the oven at 300 degrees for 30 to 45 minutes or until hard.
5. Store extra dough in an airtight container or ziplock bag.

CONCOCTION TIPS & IDEAS:

◆ Use 3/4 cup of warm coffee instead of water for an even more fragrant dough.
◆ Preserve your Java Dough sculpture by adding 1 or 2 coats of shellac.

COTTON CLAY

With this concoction, you can create snowmen and other snow-like sculptures all year around.

WHAT YOU WILL NEED:

3 cups cotton balls
2 cups water
2/3 cup flour

HOW TO CONCOCT IT:

1. Tear cotton balls apart into small pieces. Mix water and cotton balls together in a medium saucepan.
2. Slowly stir in flour. Continue stirring and cook over low heat for 5 to 7 minutes until the mixture begins to stiffen.
3. Remove saucepan from heat and place the Cotton Clay on a thick cloth towel or several layers of paper towels to cool.
4. Form Cotton Clay sculptures and allow to dry 24 hours or until hard.

CONCOCTION TIPS & IDEAS:

◆ Use Cotton Clay to create 3-D holiday snow sculptures.
◆ Cotton Clay can also be used like papier-mâché. Try molding some Cotton Clay around small boxes, bottles, and balloons.

INSTANT VOLCANO

This amazing concoction begins with a fizz, then erupts in a bubbling flow of lava.

WHAT YOU WILL NEED:

2 small paper cups
1/4 cup baking soda
1/4 cup vinegar
Red food coloring

HOW TO CONCOCT IT:

1. Fill the bottom of one small paper cup with 1/4 cup baking soda and set it on a plate.
2. Place 4 to 6 drops of red food coloring on top of the baking soda.
3. Poke a hole, about the size of a dime, in the bottom of the second paper cup.
4. Place the second paper cup upside down over the paper cup filled with baking soda.
5. Pour vinegar into the hole until the volcano begins to erupt. The more vinegar you pour into the hole, the more foam the volcano will erupt.

CONCOCTION TIPS & IDEAS:

◆ Create a fantasy volcano by adding 4 to 6 drops of blue or green food coloring and 1 tsp. of fine glitter to the baking soda.
◆ Use markers and paints to decorate the paper cups to look like real volcanoes.

JIGGLE FINGER PAINTS

This great-smelling concoction shimmers, shakes, and tickles your fingertips as you paint.

WHAT YOU WILL NEED:

1 package (3 oz.) flavored sugar-free gelatin
2 Tbs. hot water
Freezer paper (Paint on the shiny side.)

HOW TO CONCOCT IT:

1. With the help of a parent, mix gelatin and water together in a small bowl. Do not overmix!
2. Let Jiggle Finger Paints cool 5 to 10 minutes before using.
3. Jiggle Finger Paints will dry completely in 24 hours.

CONCOCTION TIPS & IDEAS:

◆ You can create unscented Jiggle Finger Paints by mixing 1 package of unflavored gelatin with 2 Tbs. of hot water and 4 to 6 drops of food coloring.

JEWEL & GEM GOOP

Mold this strange concoction into sparkling creations that look just like real jewels and gems.

WHAT YOU WILL NEED:

1/2 cup white glue
2 cups rock salt
Food coloring

HOW TO CONCOCT IT:

1. Mix rock salt and 6 to 8 drops of food coloring together.
   Add glue and continue mixing for 2 to 3 minutes.
2. Mold and sculpt Jewel & Gem Goop, using your hands.
3. Place Jewel & Gem sculptures on a piece of cardboard to dry. Drying time will vary
   according to the size and thickness of your creation.

CONCOCTION TIPS & IDEAS:

◆ Spoon Jewel & Gem Goop into plastic cookie cutters to create sparkling gems in a wide variety of shapes and sizes.
◆ Use Jewel & Gem Goop to create sparkling jewelry, holiday ornaments, or even make-believe secret treasures.

INSTANT WATERCOLORS

Here's one of the quickest, easiest, and least expensive watercolor recipes you will ever find.

WHAT YOU WILL NEED:

Food coloring
2 Tbs. water

HOW TO CONCOCT IT:

1. Mix water and 5 to 7 drops of food coloring together in a small container until completely blended.
2. Repeat the above process to create different colors of paint.

CONCOCTION TIPS & IDEAS:

◆ Use Instant Watercolors as you would any other type of watercolor paint.

TUBTIME CRAYONS

With *Tubtime Crayons*, you can color on the side of the bathtub or on tile walls and floors.

WHAT YOU WILL NEED:

1 cup grated Ivory soap
1/4 cup warm water
Food coloring
Plastic cookie cutters

HOW TO CONCOCT IT:

1. Mix water, soap, and 4 to 6 drops of food coloring together in a medium bowl. Stir the crayon mixture until it begins to harden.
2. Remove the mixture from the bowl and knead until it is the consistency of a very thick dough.
3. Spoon crayon mixture into plastic cookie cutters.
4. Place the plastic cookie cutters in the freezer for 10 minutes.
5. Pop the crayons out of the cookie cutters and allow them to dry overnight or until hard.

CONCOCTION TIPS & IDEAS:

◆ Use a plastic ice cube tray in place of cookie cutters as a mold for your Tubtime Crayons.
◆ You can also use Tubtime Crayons as bath soap.

EASY EGG MARBLEIZING

This concoction lets you create beautiful marbleized eggs in just minutes.

WHAT YOU WILL NEED:

1 Tbs. food coloring
1 Tbs. vinegar
1 Tbs. cooking oil
Hard-boiled eggs
Water

HOW TO CONCOCT IT:

1. Combine food coloring, oil, and vinegar in a small bowl until blended.
2. Add enough water to make the liquid deep enough to cover an egg.
3. Swirl the liquid around with a spoon. Quickly lower an egg into the solution and remove.
4. Pat the egg dry with a paper towel.
5. Repeat the above process, using a different color of food coloring.
6. Leave a little bit of oil on the egg to give it a varnished look.

CONCOCTION TIPS & IDEAS:

◆ Draw a design on your egg with a white crayon before dipping. The dye will not stick to your design.
◆ Use hollow eggs that have been blown out instead of hard-boiled eggs.

CRAFTY CLAY

Crafty Clay is perfect for creating detailed pieces such as beads and small figures.

WHAT YOU WILL NEED:

1 cup cornstarch
1 1/4 cups cold water
2 cups baking soda

HOW TO CONCOCT IT:

1. Combine cornstarch and baking soda in a small saucepan.
2. Add water and stir until the mixture is smooth.
3. Heat mixture for 5 minutes over medium heat. Stir until it begins to thicken and turns to dough.
4. Remove dough from saucepan and allow it to cool.
5. Knead dough 2 to 3 minutes. Let finished creations air-dry until hard.

CONCOCTION TIPS & IDEAS:

◆ Add color to your Crafty Clay by mixing in 7 to 10 drops of food coloring before cooking.
◆ Knead in 1 tsp. of fine glitter to make your Crafty Clay sculptures sparkle.

SAND CASTLE CLAY

With this concoction, you can create sand castles and sand sculptures that are permanent.

WHAT YOU WILL NEED:

1 cup sand
1/2 cup cornstarch
3/4 cup liquid starch

HOW TO CONCOCT IT:

1. Combine sand and cornstarch in an old pot.
2. Add liquid starch and mix.
3. With the help of a parent, cook the mixture over medium heat while constantly stirring.
   Eventually, the mixture will thicken and turn into dough.
4. Remove pot from the stove and let Sand Castle Clay cool.
5. Remove clay from the pot and knead it 20 to 30 seconds before using.
   Let Sand Castle Clay sculptures dry until hard.

CONCOCTION TIPS & IDEAS:

◆ Color Sand Castle Clay by adding 1 Tbs. of powdered tempera paint to the mixture before cooking.
◆ Use candy molds and cookie cutters to shape Sand Castle Clay.

JUGGLE BALLS

Practice becoming a juggling expert with these clever and durable Juggle Balls.

WHAT YOU WILL NEED:

1 small plastic bag
1/2 cup dried beans
2 medium-sized balloons

HOW TO CONCOCT IT:

1. Fill a small plastic bag with dried beans until it is the size of a juggle ball.
2. Cut the narrow end off both balloons.
3. Stretch one balloon around the plastic bag full of dried beans.
4. Stretch the remaining balloon around the bag in the opposite direction of the first balloon.

CONCOCTION TIPS & IDEAS:

◆ Decorate and personalize your Juggle Balls by using assorted felt-tipped markers.
◆ Try filling your Juggle Balls with other ingredients like dried rice, sand, or salt.

FANTASTIC FINGER PAINT

This classic finger paint recipe is the perfect rainy-day concoction.

WHAT YOU WILL NEED:

1 cup flour
2 Tbs. salt
1 1/2 cups cold water
1 1/4 cups hot water
Food coloring
Freezer paper (Paint on the shiny side.)

HOW TO CONCOCT IT:

1. Combine flour, salt, and cold water in a saucepan. Beat with a wire whisk until smooth.
2. With the help of a parent, heat the mixture over medium heat. Slowly stir in hot water.
3. Continue stirring until the mixture boils and begins to thicken. Remove from heat.
4. Beat with a whisk until smooth.
5. Divide the mixture into several different containers. Add 4 to 5 drops of food coloring to each container and stir.

CONCOCTION TIPS & IDEAS:

◆ Finger paint without getting your hands messy by placing a piece of plastic wrap over freezer paper with the finger paint between the layers.
◆ Finger paint on plastic bowls and cups. It's lots of fun, and when you're finished, the paint washes away.

3-D PUFFY SAND

Create unique 3-D paintings that dry to a rock-like finish.

WHAT YOU WILL NEED:

1/3 cup flour
1/3 cup water
1/3 cup salt
2 1/2 Tbs. tempera paint
1/2 Tbs. sand
Plastic squeeze bottle

HOW TO CONCOCT IT:

1. Combine dry ingredients in a medium bowl.
2. Add water and tempera paint. Mix until well-blended.
3. Carefully pour the mixture into a plastic squeeze bottle and paint your designs.
4. Let finished 3-D Puffy Sand paintings dry 24 hours or until hard.

CONCOCTION TIPS & IDEAS:

◆ Place 3-D Puffy Sand into a cake-decorating bag and use different tips to create cool effects and textures.
◆ Use 3-D Puffy Sand to decorate picture frames, jewelry boxes, lunch boxes, and greeting cards.

SPRAY CHALK

This washable spray paint works on sidewalks, in the snow, or on the sand.

WHAT YOU WILL NEED:

4 Tbs. cornstarch
1 cup warm water
Food coloring
1 small plant mister

HOW TO CONCOCT IT:

1. Mix cornstarch, water, and 4 to 6 drops of food coloring together in a medium bowl.
2. Pour the Spray Chalk mixture into a small plant mister. Shake and spray.
3. Avoid clogging by shaking the plant mister before each use.

CONCOCTION TIPS & IDEAS:

◆ Use Spray Chalk at the beach to paint colorful sand sculptures, on sidewalks to create graffiti-type art, or in the snow to create dazzling winter rainbows and colorful snowmen.

POSTER PAINT

This bright-colored paint is wonderful for painting posters , signs, and banners.

WHAT YOU WILL NEED:

1/4 cup flour
1 cup water
3 Tbs. powdered tempera paint
1/2 tsp. liquid starch

HOW TO CONCOCT IT:

1. Mix flour and water together in a saucepan. Stir until smooth.
2. Heat over low heat until the mixture begins to thicken.
   Remove from heat and let cool.
3. Pour the mixture into a small bowl. Add powdered tempera and liquid starch.
   Stir until completely blended.
4. Store poster paint in an airtight container.

CONCOCTION TIPS & IDEAS:

◆ Poster Paint works well on cardboard and paper surfaces. You can even use it to paint papier-mâché sculptures.
◆ Give Poster Paint a pleasant scent by adding 1 Tbs. of peppermint or any other extract.

SALTY MAP DOUGH

This concoction, combined with a little creativity, is the perfect recipe for creating an A+ salt map.

WHAT YOU WILL NEED:

1 1/2 cups flour
1 1/2 cups salt
1 1/8 cups water
Tempera paints (optional)

HOW TO CONCOCT IT:

1. Mix flour and salt together in a large bowl.
2. Slowly stir in water until the mixture is the consistency of bread dough.
3. Salty Map Dough should be used immediately.
4. Allow your finished Salty Map Dough creations to dry for 48 hours.

CONCOCTION TIPS & IDEAS:

◆ Create the ultimate salt map by using 3-D Puffy Sand to create details such as rivers, lakes, and mountains.
◆ Use assorted colors of tempera paints to paint your salty map.

GLOSSY PAINT

Create a quality, high-gloss paint in just seconds, using nothing more than common kitchen ingredients.

WHAT YOU WILL NEED:

1/2 cup condensed milk
Food coloring

HOW TO CONCOCT IT:

1. Mix condensed milk and 6 to 8 drops of food coloring together in a small bowl until completely blended.
2. Repeat the above process several times to create different colors of Glossy Paint.

CONCOCTION TIPS & IDEAS:

◆ Glossy Paint can also be used as a high-gloss finger paint.
◆ Use 1 Tbs. of liquid tempera paint in place of food coloring to create Glossy Paint in even brighter colors.

APPLESAUCE-CINNAMON DOUGH

This extremely fragrant dough has a very unique texture.

WHAT YOU WILL NEED:

1/2 cup cinnamon
1/2 cup applesauce
Plastic ziplock bag

HOW TO CONCOCT IT:

1. Pour cinnamon and applesauce into a ziplock bag.
2. Seal the ziplock bag and knead until the mixture turns to dough.
3. Allow your Applesauce-Cinnamon Dough creations to air-dry for 12 hours or until hard.

CONCOCTION TIPS & IDEAS:

◆ Roll some dough out about 1/4-inch thick. Then use cookie cutters to create fragrant tree ornaments, package ties, and air fresheners. Make a small hole toward the top of your cut-out before the dough dries so that it can be hung with string or ribbon.
◆ Applesauce-Cinnamon Dough can also be molded by pushing it into candy and popcorn molds.

WACKY WATERCOLORS

This concoction begins with a fizz and eventually transforms into hard cakes of watercolor paint.

WHAT YOU WILL NEED:

3 Tbs. baking soda
3 Tbs. cornstarch
3 Tbs. white vinegar
1 1/2 tsp. light corn syrup
Food coloring

HOW TO CONCOCT IT:

1. Mix vinegar, baking soda, cornstarch, and corn syrup together in a small bowl.
2. Divide the mixture into several small plastic tubs or jar lids.
3. Add 6 to 8 drops of food coloring to each tub or lid, and mix.
4. Use Wacky Watercolors as they are, or allow them to dry into hard cakes of paint. When painting with dry paint cakes, be sure to wet your brush before painting.

CONCOCTION TIPS & IDEAS:

◆ Experiment by mixing different colors of food coloring to create custom-blended colors of Wacky Watercolors.
◆ Use Wacky Watercolors with a pencil and a coloring book to create your own paint-by-number pictures.

SUPER SCHOOL GLUE

This homemade concoction is an inexpensive alternative to store-bought school glue.

WHAT YOU WILL NEED:

3/4 cup water
2 Tbs. corn syrup
1 tsp. white vinegar
1/2 cup cornstarch
3/4 cup ice-cold water

HOW TO CONCOCT IT:

1. Mix water, corn syrup, and vinegar together in a small saucepan until smooth.
2. Heat the mixture over medium heat until it reaches a rolling boil.
3. In a small bowl, mix cornstarch and cold water together.
   Slowly add this mixture to the first mixture. Stir until well-blended.
4. Remove saucepan from heat and allow the glue to cool.
5. Let the glue set overnight before using. Store in an airtight container.

CONCOCTION TIPS & IDEAS:

◆ Use Super School Glue as you would use any store-bought school glue.
◆ Add a little pizzazz to your Super School Glue by mixing in 4 to 6 drops of food coloring.

DOGGY TREATS

Now you can easily create cool and tasty treats that your favorite canine friend will love.

WHAT YOU WILL NEED:

2 cups whole wheat flour
1/4 cup cornmeal
1/2 cup Parmesan cheese
1 medium egg
1 cup water

HOW TO CONCOCT IT:

1. Mix all ingredients together, except the 1/4 cup of Parmesan cheese.
   Knead until thoroughly mixed.
2. Roll the dough mixture into 3-inch, pencil-sized sticks.
3. Roll the dog treats in the remaining Parmesan cheese.
4. If you are making stick-shaped treats, twist the sticks 3 to 4 times.
   Then place the treats on an ungreased baking sheet.
5. Bake at 350 degrees for 25 to 30 minutes.
6. Store dog treats in an airtight container. One batch yields 18 to 20 small treats.

CONCOCTION TIPS & IDEAS:

◆ Use cookie cutters to create Doggy Treats in the shape of animals or dog bones.
◆ Knead in 8 to 10 drops of food coloring to add variety to your treats.

SNOW PAINT

With Snow Paint, you can have fun creating colorful pictures and designs in the snow without harming the environment.

WHAT YOU WILL NEED:

1 cup water
Food coloring
1 small plant mister

HOW TO CONCOCT IT:

1. Pour water into a small plant mister.
2. Add 10 to 12 drops of food coloring. Screw the spray top back on the plant mister and shake.
3. Repeat the above process to create Snow Paint in a variety of colors.

CONCOCTION TIPS & IDEAS:

◆ Make a snowman or a snow angel. Then use Snow Paint to create faces and clothing for your snow creations.
◆ Use Snow Paint to create messages or banners in the snow.

COMIC COPIER SOLUTION

With this concoction, you can make a copy of any black-and-white or colored newspaper photograph.

WHAT YOU WILL NEED:

1 tsp. vanilla extract
1 tsp. liquid dish detergent
Comic strip or newspaper picture
White paper

HOW TO CONCOCT IT:

1. Mix vanilla extract and liquid dish detergent together in a small bowl.
2. Using your finger or a small paint brush, completely cover the comic or newspaper picture with a thin layer of Comic Copier Solution.
3. Place a clean sheet of white paper on top of the picture. Firmly rub the back of the paper with a spoon until the picture begins to show through the paper.
4. Peel the paper off the picture to see your Comic Copier creation.

CONCOCTION TIPS & IDEAS:

◆ Use the Comic Copier Solution to create greeting cards and wrapping paper.
◆ Comic Copier Solution can also be used to create cool book covers or lunch bags.

SHAKE & MAKE ICE CREAM

Prepare this ice-cold, tasty treat in just a few short minutes.

WHAT YOU WILL NEED:

2 Tbs. sugar
1 cup milk or half-and-half
1/2 tsp. vanilla
6 Tbs. rock salt
1 pint-sized plastic ziplock bag
1 gallon-sized plastic ziplock bag

HOW TO CONCOCT IT:

1. Fill the gallon-sized ziplock bag half full with ice. Add rock salt and seal.
2. Pour sugar, milk or half-and-half, and vanilla into the pint-sized plastic bag and seal.
3. Place the pint-sized ziplock bag into the gallon-sized ziplock bag and seal.
4. Shake the bag for 5 to 7 minutes.
5. Open the small ziplock bag and enjoy!

CONCOCTION TIPS & IDEAS:

◆ Make peppermint ice cream by adding 1/2 tsp. peppermint extract or 3 Tbs. of crushed peppermint stick.
◆ Try topping your ice cream with sprinkles, nuts, or fresh fruit.

STICKY PAINT

Sticky Paint's smooth texture and rich color make it the perfect paint for very young artists.

WHAT YOU WILL NEED:

2 Tbs. light corn syrup
Food coloring

HOW TO CONCOCT IT:

1. Mix corn syrup and 4 to 6 drops of food coloring together in a small bowl until well-blended.
2. Repeat the above process to create different colors of Sticky Paint.

CONCOCTION TIPS & IDEAS:

◆ Sticky Paint also makes a wonderful finger paint.
◆ Substitute 1 tsp. of liquid tempera paint in place of food coloring to create even more vivid colors.

ROCK CANDY

This tasty homemade treat has been a favorite of children around the world for many decades.

WHAT YOU WILL NEED:

2 cups water
4 cups sugar

HOW TO CONCOCT IT:

1. Pour water into a large saucepan.
2. Add sugar and stir for 2 to 3 minutes to dissolve as much sugar as possible.
3. Place the saucepan on the stove on medium to medium-high heat.
4. Continue to stir the solution until all of the sugar is dissolved.
5. Remove the saucepan from the stove and allow the liquid to cool.
6. Pour the mixture into a square plastic container.
7. In 7 to 10 days the bottom of your container will be covered with Rock Candy.
8. Turn the plastic container upside down in a sink and allow it to drain for one hour.
9. Break the Rock Candy up into chunks and place it on several layers of paper towels to dry.

CONCOCTION TIPS & IDEAS:

◆ Before cooking, add food coloring to your sugar mixture to create edible Rock Candy gems that look like rubies, emeralds, and sapphires.
◆ Place different colors of Rock Candy in a jar to create a colorful candy art gift.

WALK OF FAME STONES

Use Walk of Fame Stones to bring a touch of Hollywood to your backyard or garden.

WHAT YOU WILL NEED:

Old bucket
8 cups quick-setting cement
Water
Shallow cardboard box (11 x 16 works best)
Stick or pencil
Old Ruler

HOW TO CONCOCT IT:

1. Mix cement and 2 cups of water together in a bucket until the mixture is the consistency of oatmeal. Add more cement or water if necessary.
2. Pour the mixture evenly into the cardboard box. Your cement should be at least 1 1/2 to 2 inches thick.
3. Take an old ruler and rake across the top of the cement until smooth. Wait 5 minutes.
4. Place your hands or feet into the wet cement and push down 1 to 2 inches to make your impression. Immediately rinse your hands/feet with water.
5. Use a stick or pencil to write your name, age, or date in the cement.
6. Let the cement dry for 48 hours. Tear away the cardboard box and place your Walk of Fame Stone in your backyard or garden.

CONCOCTION TIPS & IDEAS:

◆ Personalize your Walk of Fame Stone by adding seashells, toy cars, marbles, coins, dominoes, old jewelry, etc.

FLOWER PETAL CLAY

Flower Petal Clay is a beautiful, natural clay that you can use to create small treasures in a rainbow of swirling colors.

WHAT YOU WILL NEED:

1/2 cup flour
1 Tbs. salt
3 Tbs. water
3 cups finely chopped and crushed fresh flower petals

HOW TO CONCOCT IT:

1. Mix flour, salt, and water together in a small bowl until it forms a firm dough.
2. Knead in flower petals.
3. Wrap dough in plastic wrap and put it in the refrigerator for 20 minutes. Now you're ready to create!
4. Let finished pieces air-dry 2 to 3 days or until completely hard. You can apply a thin layer of shellac to preserve and add luster to your Flower Petal Clay creations.

CONCOCTION TIPS & IDEAS:

◆ With Flower Petal Clay, you can create beautiful beads in many shapes and sizes. Use a toothpick to poke a hole in your beads while they are still wet. After your beads are dried, you can string them to form unique bracelets, necklaces, or tree garlands.

CRYSTAL ROCK GARDEN

Grow beautiful multi-colored crystals, using just a few simple household ingredients.

WHAT YOU WILL NEED:

1 small sponge
4 Tbs. salt
2 Tbs. water
2 Tbs. liquid bluing
Food coloring
Rubber gloves

HOW TO CONCOCT IT:

1. Cut sponge into several small pieces. Place sponge pieces in a small plastic or glass bowl.
2. Put on rubber gloves, sprinkle 2 Tbs. salt, water, and liquid bluing over the sponge pieces. Allow the concoction to set for 24 hours.
3. Sprinkle the remaining 2 Tbs. of salt over the sponge pieces. Allow the concoction to set for an additional 24 hours.
4. Repeat step 2. Then add a few drops of food coloring to each sponge piece. By this time your crystal flower garden should be starting to bloom.

CONCOCTION TIPS & IDEAS:

◆ You can use cotton balls, coal, or porous brick pieces in place of a sponge to create your Crystal Rock Garden.
◆ Crystal Rock Garden is a great science experiment that demonstrates how crystals form and grow.

FRUITY PLAY DOUGH

This soft, pliable play dough is as much fun to smell as it is to sculpt and mold.

WHAT YOU WILL NEED:

2 1/4 cups flour
1 cup salt
2 Tbs. unsweetened powdered drink mix
4 Tbs. cooking oil
1 cup water

HOW TO CONCOCT IT:

1. Combine flour, salt, and powdered drink mix in a large bowl.
2. Stir in cooking oil and water.
3. Continue stirring until mixture is the consistency of bread dough.
4. Remove dough from bowl and knead on a floured surface 2 to 3 minutes until firm.

CONCOCTION TIPS & IDEAS:

◆ Mold different Fruity Play Dough colors/scents into pieces of make-believe fruit. Just make sure you don't eat them!
◆ Store leftover Fruity Play Dough in an airtight container or plastic ziplock bag.

CRAZY CRITTERS

You'll have hours of fun creating, decorating, and naming your very own Crazy Critters pets.

WHAT YOU WILL NEED:

1/3 cup quick-setting plaster of Paris
5 Tbs. water
Balloons of assorted sizes
Funnel with a large opening
1 Tbs. tempera paint or 5 to 7 drops of food coloring
Supplies to decorate critters: paint, glue, glitter, google eyes, feathers, etc.

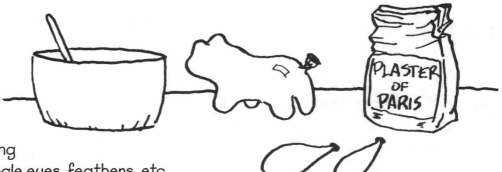

HOW TO CONCOCT IT:

1. Blow up a balloon as large as possible. Clamp the end of the balloon shut with a paper clip or clothespin. Allow it to stretch for 5 to 10 minutes.
2. Deflate the balloon and attach it to the funnel.
3. Mix water, plaster, and paint or food coloring together until smooth. Pour plaster mixture into the balloon. Remove the funnel and tie balloon shut.
4. Stretch the balloon into any shape and hold it until plaster begins to become firm.
5. Let the balloon set for 1 hour.
6. Tear balloon off the plaster shape. Then paint or decorate your Crazy Critters.

CONCOCTION TIPS & IDEAS:

◆ Crazy Critters make interesting and versatile conversation pieces that can be used for anything from a paperweight to an imaginary pet.

COOL CRAYONS

Create some of the coolest crayons you've ever seen with this simple recycling recipe.

WHAT YOU WILL NEED:

Broken crayons
Heavy paper cups
Assorted candy molds
Oven mitt

HOW TO CONCOCT IT:

1. Remove all paper from crayons and sort by color in heavy paper cups.
2. Place one cup of crayons into a microwave oven. Cook on high for 4 to 6 minutes or until the crayons are completely melted.
3. Using an oven mitt, have an adult carefully pour the melted crayon wax into candy molds. Throw the used paper cup away.
4. Place the candy molds in the freezer for 20 minutes until the wax is hard.
5. Pop Cool Crayons out of the candy molds and color.

CONCOCTION TIPS & IDEAS:

◆ Try melting 2 to 3 different colors of crayons together to create marbleized crayons.
◆ If your microwave has a glass tray, let it cool down after 15 minutes of use. The tray must be allowed to cool one hour to prevent burns to the user, and to prevent damage to the glass tray.
◆ Heavy paper cups must be microwave safe.

TREASURE STONES

These stones can be broken open to reveal hidden treasures and secret messages.

WHAT YOU WILL NEED:

1 cup flour
1 cup used coffee grinds
1/2 cup salt
1/4 cup sand
3/4 cup water

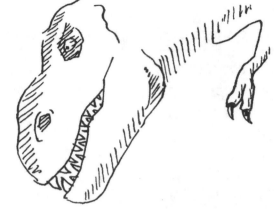

HOW TO CONCOCT IT:

1. Mix flour, coffee grinds, salt, and sand together in a medium bowl.
2. Slowly add water and knead until the mixture is the consistency of bread dough.
3. Break off a piece of dough and roll it into the size of a baseball.
4. Make a hole in the center of the ball big enough to hide treasures in.
5. Fill the hole with treasures and seal with extra dough.
6. Let your Treasure Stones air-dry for 2 to 3 days or until hard, or bake in the oven on a cookie sheet at 150 degrees for 15 to 20 minutes.

CONCOCTION TIPS & IDEAS:

◆ Add 1 Tbs. of powdered tempera paint to tint your Treasure Stones different colors.
◆ Use Treasure Stones for party favors or scavenger hunts at your next party.

Index